Contents

SWEET MUSIC!

Have you ever daydreamed about spending your life playing and making music? If so, you're not alone. At some point, almost all of us have imagined family, friends or even crowds going wild for us as we perform songs we've written.

Whether or not you already play an instrument, you can make music! All you need is time, dedication and a handful of great ideas!

Media Genius

CREATE YOUR OWN

MUSIC

Matt Anniss

Raintree is an imprint of Capstone Global Library Limited, a company incorporated in England and Wales having its registered office at 264 Banbury Road, Oxford, OX2 7DY – Registered company number: 6695582

www.raintree.co.uk
myorders@raintree.co.uk

Edited by James Benefield and Helen Cox Cannons
Designed by Steve Mead
Original illustrations © Capstone Global Library Ltd 2016
Picture research by Morgan Walters
Production by Victoria Fitzgerald
Originated by Capstone Global Library
Printed and bound in China

ISBN 978 1 474 71376 4 (hardback)
20 19 18 17 16
10 9 8 7 6 5 4 3 2 1

ISBN 978 1 474 71385 6 (paperback)
21 20 19 18 17
10 9 8 7 6 5 4 3 2 1

British Library Cataloguing in Publication Data
A full catalogue record for this book is available from the British Library.

Acknowledgements
We would like to thank the following for permission to reproduce photographs: Alamy: Anatolii Babii, 26, Marc Tielemans, top 28; Corbis: Rune Hellestad, 30; Dreamstime: Petr Malyshev, bottom 29, Yuri Snow, 20; Getty Images: Alex Robinson, 7, Bennett Raglin/BET, 21, Fred Hayes, 38, Future Music Magazine, 18, Gabriel Olsen, 37, Girl Ray, cover, Jeff Kravitz, 31, Johnny Nunez/Contributor, bottom 9, PYMCA, 32, Tim Mosenfelder, middle 11, 34; Newscom: Daily Mirror Mirrorpix, 8, Dan Cappellazzo/Polaris, top right 9, DC5/Dominic Chan/WENN, 17, KEIZO MORI, 6; Shutterstock: antb, 25, bikeriderlondon, 24, DFree, top 11, Everett Collection, 43, FashionStock.com, 5, Featureflash, 19, Fenton one, top left 29, Iaremenko Sergii, bottom 28, JStone, 23, Kaspri, 9, Mat Hayward, 40, Monkey Business Images, 4, Moo teaforthree, 41, Pavel L Photo and Video, spread 12-13, Seksan44, middle 28, spline_x, 14, Stokkete, bottom 11, 22, totally out, 33; Wikimedia: Matt Vanacoro, top right 29

We would like to thank Patrick Allen for his invaluable help in the preparation of this book.

Every effort has been made to contact copyright holders of material reproduced in this book. Any omissions will be rectified in subsequent printings if notice is given to the publisher.

All the internet addresses (URLs) given in this book were valid at the time of going to press. However, due to the dynamic nature of the internet, some addresses may have changed, or sites may have changed or ceased to exist since publication. While the author and publisher regret any inconvenience this may cause readers, no responsibility for any such changes can be accepted by either the author or the publisher.

Success Story

Ed Sheeran is a great example of what can be achieved with dedication and talent. He began writing and playing his own songs on the guitar when he was 11. His music career began to take off after he spent a summer in London when he was 14, playing concerts for little or no money. Over the next six years, he recorded and released his own CDs and downloads, building up a massive fan base. By the time he was 21, he was a global music megastar.

Even if the idea of playing in bands to crowds of people doesn't excite you, you may still want to make music. Perhaps you're more interested in creating music with friends, performing in a singing group or making music on a computer, laying down beats for rappers. How about helping others fulfil their dreams by becoming a music producer? No matter how you want to get started, this book will provide you with the inspiration you need.

Just do it!

Today, creating music is easier than ever. You could sing with friends, learn an instrument or join an orchestra. Thanks to mobile electronics and computer software, you could now make music on a computer or smartphone, even if you can't play an instrument. When it comes to creating music, the options are almost endless!

CHAPTER 1

What's your SOUND?

One of the greatest things about music is the sheer number of different styles to enjoy. Each of these styles, sometimes called genres, can be created in countless different ways. You may have heard and be able to identify some of these styles: the orchestra-led sound of classical music, the guitar-heavy strut of rock, or the heavy drumbeats of electronic dance music (also known as EDM, club or dance music). This is not to mention the variety of music from other cultures and countries.

Head to the UK's National Festival of Music for Youth, and you'll find children performing many different types of music.

You can often find music being performed by buskers on street corners. They try to brighten our lives with music in exchange for a little bit of money.

All around us

If you're going to create music, it's helpful to know about different styles and the ways they are sometimes used. Music is created, performed, recorded and used for many different purposes. In the last few days, you may have come across:

- popular songs drifting from the radio, played to entertain listeners
- music in the background of films and television shows, designed to enhance the action on-screen
- music used on advertisements, made to sell products. Sometimes this is created for the adverts; sometimes advertisers use already-existing music.
- people singing religious songs, as an expression of their faith
- light music being played in public places (sometimes known as Muzak), to provide a soundtrack to your shopping experience.

THE KNOWLEDGE

In 2014, journalists working for *Time* magazine determined the most played song of all time. They believe that it is "It's A Small World", which is famous for being performed at Disney theme parks. *Time* estimates that it has been played more than 50 million times since 1964!

Learning from cover versions

An interesting way of discovering some of the different ways music can be used and interpreted is to listen to some "cover versions" of the same song. These are interpretations of a popular song, often in different styles from the original version. Covers usually retain key elements of the song, such as the melody and the lyrics. Around these, the musicians will change one or more of the following:

- the way the lyrics are performed
- the instruments used in the song
- the pattern of drumbeats used in the backing track
- the speed, or tempo, the song is performed
- the style of music it's performed in, for example jazz instead of pop.

To see how this works in practice, listen to some covers of one of the most famous songs of all time.

THE ORIGINAL: THE BEATLES

The Beatles' version (recorded in 1966) featured the band singing over traditional string instruments, including violin and cello, but no drumbeats. It has since been covered more than 130 times.

COVER 1: ARETHA FRANKLIN

Singer Aretha Franklin recorded a soul version of "Eleanor Rigby" in 1969. Instead of strings, she used drums and pianos. Franklin also changed the words slightly.

Comparing "ELEANOR RIGBY"

COVER 2: MARGATE

American punk rock band Margate's 2011 version features heavy drums, with the song's melody being played on guitars.

COVER 3: JA RULE

Rapper Ja Rule didn't just cover "Eleanor Rigby", he turned it into a different song, 2008's "Father Forgive Me". He retained some elements of the Beatles song, but added his own rap lyrics and hip-hop-style drumbeats.

Identify, compare and contrast

Being able to identify styles of music will help you to compare and contrast different ways of creating music. Listening to covers is just one way. Another is to actively seek out styles you may not have listened to very much, such as traditional forms of music from around the world. If you do this, you'll begin to notice the differences much more, such as the instruments used, the chords, musical scales and rhythms that feature in the songs.

Once you learn how to identify the differences between styles, you can then work out which style of music you'd like to create. You don't have to stick to one style; you could even combine the best bits of a number of genres you enjoy.

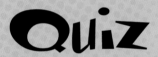

What kind of music should I create?

If you're still unsure as to which path to take, the following quiz might help...

How do you prefer to work?
A: On your own
B: Sometimes on your own and sometimes with a group of people
C: With a group of friends or other like-minded musicians

Are you interested in performing in front of people?
A: Possibly at some point
B: Not that keen
C: Definitely!

Which of the following sounds more exciting?
A: Writing, playing and singing your own songs
B: Creating music on a computer
C: Playing instruments as often as possible

IF YOU ANSWERED MOSTLY ...

A: You're suited to being a songwriter, singer or solo performer.

B: You're a born DJ, dance producer or hip-hop musician.

C: You should be in a band, orchestra or singing group. Alternatively, you could be a session musician, making guest appearances at concerts and recording sessions.

CHAPTER 2

Making music

There are almost as many ways to make music as there are different musical styles. However, you don't need special training or complicated equipment to get started. To get the ball rolling, gather together a group of friends to create some music with you.

Want to make music? You can play musical instruments in a group with your friends. Or you can go it alone and do your own thing, even without an instrument to play.

Jam on it!

Musical improvisation in a group is sometimes called jamming. Many musicians get together for "jam" sessions, where they create new songs simply through trying things out. You could try to write a song with your friends by following these steps:

1. Begin by getting somebody to create a beat. An instrument isn't needed. Try clapping, or tapping a foot on the floor.
2. Think of some lyrics to sing over the top of this beat. You could start with a simple phrase or sentence, which can be repeated in time to the beat.
3. Get one of your friends to play a sequence of musical notes that complements the melody being sung.
4. Keep the beats, lyrics and melody going at the same time. As you go along, get other friends with instruments to join in.

Pro Tip

There are now loads of free software applications, or apps, that can help you make music on a smartphone or tablet. For example, apps could help you jam out music on your guitar, make drumbeats or learn to play piano. They can also help you to produce songs from start to finish.

Once you've got these four elements, you're well on your way to composing your first song!

Using chords to create music

The process of writing a piece of music, either by jamming or another method, is known as composition. Many musicians use chords during the composition process. Chords are an important part of music; they feature heavily in many different styles.

You can make a chord yourself by playing three or more musical notes at the same time. Chords can be played on many instruments, including guitar and piano. You'll know when you've found a chord, because the notes all sound good together. Notes that sound good together are said to be in harmony.

THE KNOWLEDGE

Here are three basic piano chords. Each letter on the keyboard below corresponds to a musical note. Play the highlighted notes simultaneously to create the chord.

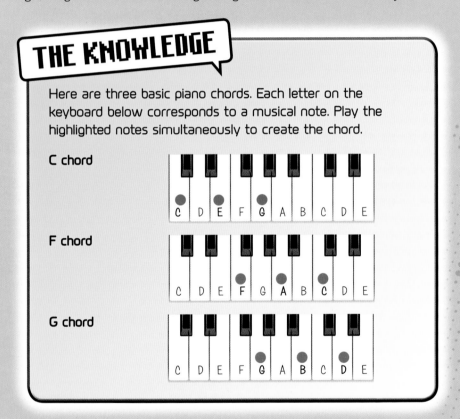

C chord

F chord

G chord

Sequences and progressions

Songs usually contain a number of chords played one after another in succession. This is known as a chord sequence or a chord progression. You can create great sequences with just a handful of chords. Try to create some chord sequences using the three chords shown above. How many can you find? If you find a sequence that you think sounds good, write it down. You can use the letters that correspond to the chords, for example C, F, G. Or, if you are using a guitar, use a guitar tab.

Chord sequences on a guitar are often written down using something called guitar tab. Each chord is represented on a grid. The grid shows the guitarist which strings to hold down along the fretboard, or the neck, of the guitar. You can find lots of good advice about, and examples of, chords and guitar tabs online.

C chord

This indicates the nut, or top of the fretboard.

The horizontal lines indicate the dividers between the frets.

The red dots indicate where you should place your fingers on the fretboard.

Don't strum the strings marked with a cross.

A circle indicates an "open string" (a string that isn't pressed anywhere on the fretboard during a chord).

The vertical lines indicate the six strings on a guitar – the one furthest left is bottom string, the one furthest right is top string (in terms of pitch).

Writing songs

The process of composing a song is known as songwriting. Songwriters combine melodies and chords with lyrics. In some ways, songs are like poems set to music. They tell a story or talk about something by following a simple structure, usually alternating between verses and choruses.

Verses are used to tell the story of the song. They usually consist of between four and eight sentences, which often rhyme. The melody of each verse is usually the same throughout the song, but the words are different each time.

Choruses are often the most memorable part of the song. They can be the part that you're most likely to sing along to. Choruses usually contain the main message, and are repeated several times throughout the song. A song's chorus may have a different melody to the verses.

In addition, songwriters usually start songs using a short musical introduction. This is known as an intro and it is designed to catch the attention of listeners. The song may finish with an ending called the outro.

Try it yourself!

Try writing your own song. If you're stuck for inspiration, write about your day, or how you're feeling. You could use the following basic structure:

Intro → Verse 1 → Chorus → Verse 2 → Chorus → Outro

As you write your song, make a note of the chords you'll be using as well as the lyrics. Some songwriters do this by writing the name of the chord above the point in the song where it should be played, as shown in this example:

Baa Baa Black Sheep

G   C   G
Baa Baa Black Sheep, have you any wool?

C   G   D   G
Yes Sir, Yes Sir, three bags full.

G   C   G   D
One for the master, one for the dame,

Singer-songwriters such as Jamie T are skilled at combining great chord progressions and melodies with thoughtful lyrics.

Today, creating songs is very easy, thanks to computer software and modern music technology.

Making music with computers

If you can't play musical instruments, don't worry. You can still make music, thanks to computer technology. You don't need much kit to start with, and there's loads of useful information online to help beginners.

Sorting out software

The first thing you'll need to write a song with a computer is, of course, access to a computer. Once you've got that sorted, you'll need to get hold of a Digital Audio Workstation (DAW), sometimes also called a sequencer. This is a piece of software that allows you to write, record and produce music, all through one on-screen interface.

There are loads of DAW packages available. Some are complex, but there are also plenty that are suitable for beginners. Many of these are either completely free or cheap, or offer you a free trial. Good options for beginners include GarageBand, Ableton Live, Reaper, Studio One Free and Podium Free.

Along with a DAW, you might also find it useful to get hold of a MIDI controller keyboard. These keyboards plug into your computer and will allow you to play notes and chords. They also control many other aspects of the music-making process.

Success Story

DJ, dance producer and pop star Calvin Harris started to make music in his bedroom as a young teenager. He started by using a cheap computer, simple software and keyboards he'd borrowed from school. This equipment helped him to slowly learn the skills needed to make great dance tracks and, later, chart-topping pop songs. He released his first song almost exactly 10 years after he started making music.

Creating a new sound

DAWs are great because they can be used to create music in a number of different ways. For example, they feature options to change the sound of notes and chords. In other words, you can make them sound like any instrument you can think of. This flexibility gives music-makers a huge amount of control over the sound of their songs.

Varied methods

Some people use computers and DAW software to create music which sounds like it could be written by traditional songwriters. For example, they arrange songs with intros and choruses. However, other people do it very differently.

Many beginners choose to work with preset musical loops, or sounds that repeat. These loops often come free with DAW software such as GarageBand. Many of these are samples of other things. These are short snatches of sound, for example a single guitar note, drum stroke or piano chord. You can also create your own loops with bursts of drumbeats, guitar riffs, chords or melodies.

Many dance producers begin a track by tapping out a beat on a MIDI controller or drum machine, before recording it on the computer.

Sampling for beginners

Many computer musicians use samples. Some music producers create entire songs by layering different samples on top of each other and arranging them into something that sounds good together. You can download free sample packs containing different sounds from online music libraries and music technology websites.

Pro Tip

If your DAW came with loops, try creating a complete piece of music using them. Just load up a few different loops, then put them in some kind of order on-screen. When you're happy with the arrangement of the loops, you're finished!

Like many leading hip-hop producers, Timbaland extensively uses samples of other people's music in his work.

Developing your music

You've now chosen a music-making method that you're comfortable with. This could be jamming with a band, writing your own songs or creating beats on a computer. Now, you can start thinking about how to develop your music.

If you have friends who are accomplished musicians, you could get them to come up with violin, cello, saxophone or piano parts – to name a few – for your songs or instrumental tracks.

Same song, different sounds

Try playing or arranging the songs or instrumental music you've created so far in different ways. For example:

- Test out different approaches to singing, either by belting out the lyrics or delivering them softly.
- Get some friends to sing on your song. They could either sing along with the choruses, or make harmonious noises, such as "ooohs" and "aaaahs" in the background of the verses or choruses.
- Try playing the song more slowly or quickly.
- Extend the song by including an instrumental passage in the middle. A friend could play a different kind of instrument over the top of this section.
- Attempt to play the song in a different musical style, for example reggae instead of rock.
- Alter the pattern of drumbeats to give the song a different feel.

Alternatively, you could make your own cover versions of songs you like. You can often find details of the chords and lyrics of existing songs on the internet.

Success Story

Some of the most famous singers of all time didn't write their own songs. Legendary rock-and-roll star Elvis Presley employed a team of professional songwriters to write hits for him throughout the 1950s and 1960s. Many of today's biggest pop bands, including One Direction, don't write their own songs either.

CHAPTER 3

Recording music

Recording is a good place to start when you're ready to share your music with the world. You stand more chance of getting bookings to perform concerts (often called gigs) and attracting fans if you've got a smart demonstration recording. This is known in the music industry as a demo.

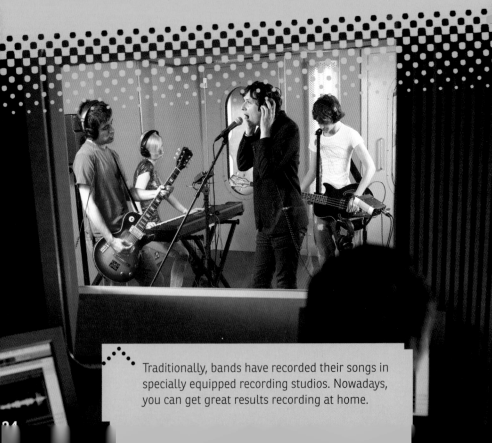

Traditionally, bands have recorded their songs in specially equipped recording studios. Nowadays, you can get great results recording at home.

Different demos

Demos can be recorded in a number of ways:

- If you're trying to capture the energy of a live performance, it makes sense to record it as you perform it, in one take. You could record the performance on your phone or tablet. Then you could transfer it to a computer to burn on a CD or you could just upload it onto the internet.
- If you want more control over how the recording sounds, you might record each individual part (singing, instruments, drums) separately, then arrange them on the computer to create the finished song. This can be done at home using a DAW or in a recording studio.
- You could compose and record your music at the same time, using a DAW, MIDI controller keyboard and non-electronic instruments, too.

Pro Tip

The final stage of the recording process is known as mixing. This is when you adjust the sound levels of each individual element of the recording (for example the guitar parts, singing and drums) with the aim of creating a brilliant-sounding finished product. Instruments and vocals are then mixed together, either on a computer or using a studio mixing desk.

25

Recording instruments

Do you want to record a piece of music with live instruments and vocals (singing, rapping or speaking)? Arguably the best way of doing this is to make a multitrack recording. Each instrument or vocal is recorded on a separate track, either using a DAW or a portable multitrack recorder.
You can also record vocals and non-electric instruments (such as drums) at the same time. This is done on a number of separate tracks, sometimes called channels.

Going solo

Multitrack recording is good for musicians who work on their own. You can record in your own time, starting with guitar or piano parts, before adding other tracks like drums and vocals later. Once you've got the hang of this kind of recording, you can finish rough recordings of songs very quickly. Many professional musicians use this to develop new songs before recording them properly in a studio.

Multitrack mixing

Portable multitrack recorders also allow you to mix your song once all the parts have been recorded. This is because you can alter the volume of each track, using one of several controls to alter the way the recording sounds. Once you've set the mix levels you can save the song as an MP3 file.

DAW software for smartphones and tablets allows you to play, record and mix songs as you go along.

Recording with mobile devices

If you've got access to a smartphone or tablet, then you can use it as a portable recording studio. Today, lots of apps exist to help you record and produce music. Some use your device's built-in microphone, while others piece together tracks from scratch using loops and samples.

A number of DAW packages, such as GarageBand, even have a mobile-friendly version; some of these are free to download from the internet. However, there are problems with recording on mobiles and tablets. Firstly, you need to have enough memory on the device to store your music and run the DAW package. Also, you will need a DAW to link to more than one microphone and other external devices you wish to plug into your computer.

Recording with computers

Recording with computers requires a little more equipment than using a portable multitrack recorder, but it gives you even more options. With DAW packages, there are few limits to the number of tracks you can record to. That means you can add and arrange as many sounds, instruments, samples, vocals and loops as you wish.

Each sound is given its own track, allowing you a huge amount of control over how it sounds. This way, you can add special effects to a sound, or change its volume, without affecting the other sounds you've used.

Multiple choice

DAW software allows you to write, record and arrange songs as you go along. It also has a number of other useful options, including:

▶	editing tools that allow you to chop down longer recordings into smaller chunks, or remove parts you don't like
▶	an "arrangement window", where you can drag and drop tracks or parts of tracks around the screen to structure your song
▶	a sampler tool to help you create short samples of sounds or other recordings
▶	a mixer for finalizing the sound levels of each track, to produce final "mix downs"
▶	the chance to "undo" something if you mess it up, or don't like an element of the recording.

MULTITRACK EQUIPMENT

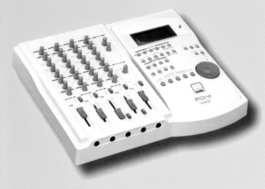

PORTABLE MULTITRACK RECORDER

Instruments and microphones are plugged into different track channels using audio leads. The number of tracks available differs from recorder to recorder, but usually ranges from 4 to 16. Alternatively, you could use a DAW.

AUDIO LEADS

These are used to plug microphones and instruments into the multitrack recorder.

MICROPHONE

This can be used to record vocals and non-electric instruments such as drums. You would plug this into the multitrack recorder with an audio lead. If you want to record on a computer using more than one microphone, you would need to use a DAW or similar.

COMPUTER RECORDING EQUIPMENT

SOUNDCARD
A soundcard is a device that acts as an interface between electronic music equipment, traditional instruments and a computer. Most musicians use an external sound card, which plugs into their computer using USB.

COMPUTER
This is the centre of the action, loaded up with your choice of DAW software.

MIDI CONTROLLER KEYBOARD
This is for playing in sounds, creating beat patterns and controlling aspects of the software.

CHAPTER 4

Performing *Music*

Many musicians will tell you that there's nothing quite like the buzz of performing live in front of an enthusiastic crowd. If you're passionate about music, there's a good chance that you too would love to feel the thrill of performing!

Singer-songwriter KT Tunstall is famous for using a loop pedal. She can sample short musical passages she plays onstage, which she then sings over.

Anyone can do it!

Once upon a time, you had to be a trained musician – skilful at playing an instrument or good at singing – to perform live. Today, there are no such boundaries. Music software enables computer musicians to play and arrange prerecorded tracks onstage before a live crowd. Electronic gadgets can help single musicians create their own musical backing tracks on the spot.

Superstar DJs, here we go!

Another way of getting the thrill of performance is to take up DJing. DJs perform sets of other people's music – and sometimes their own – by playing CDs, MP3 files or vinyl records. The best DJs mix these songs together to form a seamless musical performance. They often do this using a method called beat-matching.

The idea behind beat-matching is simple. DJs attempt to blend the drumbeats of two songs so that they're in time with each other. This creates a non-stop rhythm when switching between songs. To help them do this, they use equipment that lets them subtly change the speed of every song that they play. They also use a DJ mixer that lets them switch between two or more songs. This also helps to alter the sound levels. The result is that DJs, like Skrillex, opposite, are able to blend songs and instrumental tracks to create a seamless, non-stop performance!

Get in the mix!

DJing is a great way to get into performance, and you don't need a group of people to perform with. There are loads of software and apps for laptop computers and mobile devices allowing you to experience the thrill of mixing like a pro DJ. This kind of software is often free and you don't need to buy extra equipment. Good examples include Serato DJ Intro, Virtual DJ and DJ Studio 5.

The software and apps mentioned above allow you to load up two MP3 song files, including those you've made yourself, and mix them together. If this sounds attractive, try to get an adult to download some software for you to try out!

You could put on your own DJ party at home or school, and invite your friends to come along and dance.

Friends and family first

If you're more of a musician and want to perform onstage yourself, you need to gain experience performing live. In future you might be able to secure gigs in recognized concert venues, perhaps by giving demos to people who put on concerts in your area. First, though, you should concentrate on performing to family and friends. One way to do this is to arrange a small performance at school or in a local youth club.

If you've decided to put on your own gig, you'll need to promote it yourself. Try designing your own posters to put up at school and around the neighbourhood. Remember to include the name of the band performing, the venue, the time the concert starts and how much it costs to get in.

THE FUNKY LIZARDS

12.15 – lunch break
School Hall

FREE ENTRY

Dance act Daft Punk's reputation has been built as much on their dynamic live shows as the quality of their records.

Before the Big Day

Once you've secured your first booking from a venue, you need to make sure you're fully prepared. For starters, that means doing a lot of practice. You need to make sure you'll be able to play and sing your songs well – even if you're suffering from nerves. If you're in a band, practise together as much as possible. You should practise the songs that you want to perform over and over again until you're happy with them.

Live beats

Performing is a little different for people using computers. You still need to practise so that you're familiar with the software or electronic equipment you'll be using for your performance. Get to know it inside out. For example, plan ahead the order in which you want to trigger your loops, beats, chords and melodies.

Whether you're using instruments, computers or a combination of both, you'll still need to work out a set list. This is a list of the songs you're going to perform. Most new bands perform a mixture of their own material and cover versions of songs by well-known musicians. This set list should include enough songs to fill up your allotted time. It's a good idea to choose an extra song in case your audience asks for an encore.

Success Story

Top music acts can earn huge amounts of money from massive world tours. U2 currently hold the record for the highest earnings from a tour. Between 2009 and 2011, their 360 world tour raked in a whopping £485 million ($736 million)!

CHAPTER 5

Sharing your
MUSiC

Naturally, all musicians are proud of the music they make and want as many people as possible to hear it. It's likely that you're no different. Having recorded some songs, you want the world to sit up and take note of what you have produced.

That means sharing your music, first with family, friends and classmates, and later the world. For example, start sharing by burning some CDs and handing them out. Perhaps you could email out MP3 files or even give out portable USB sticks with some of your songs on them.

Get online!

Today, millions of musicians, bands and DJs around the world use the internet to share their music with the world. SoundCloud, one of the world's most popular websites for sharing new music, has hundreds of millions of regular users. Research supports the idea that the internet is fast becoming the most popular place for people to discover new music. According to a 2014 study by research firm Nielsen, the number of Americans listening to music over the internet has gone up by 32 per cent since 2012.

STAY SAFE

Before you upload your songs to the internet and share them with the world, make sure your parent or guardian knows what you're sharing. When using online music sharing sites, don't talk to strangers using the messaging service. You wouldn't speak to strangers in real life, and your approach to meeting people on the internet should be no different.

Singer Iza Lach got her big break internationally by entering an online music competition run by rapper Snoop Dogg. The rapper liked her entry so much that he signed her to his record label. He has since recorded a number of songs with her.

Teenage singer-songwriter Greyson Chance became an overnight internet sensation after posting a video of himself performing a Lady Gaga song on YouTube. It led to a deal with a record company, hit songs and a world tour!

Online options

There are many websites out there where you can upload your music for people to listen to, but SoundCloud and hearthis.at are by far the most popular. Both websites are remarkably easy to use, and offer very similar services. With an account, you upload and showcase your music to millions of potential listeners around the world. Before you sign up and begin the upload process, remember to get a parent or guardian's permission.

Easy uploading

The upload process on sites such as SoundCloud and YouTube is very simple. Before you start, you will need to sign up for a free account with an email address and password, before giving some details about your song and band. You're then ready to share your music!

There are a couple of ways you can get noticed on these sites. For example, you could add a short description to each new upload to entice new listeners. Also, consider uploading a picture or an artwork to accompany the song. Once you've made these choices, it's just a case of uploading the MP3 file or video, and waiting for the process to finish. Within a few minutes, you'll be able to share your song with the world, either by emailing the link to friends, putting a link on other websites or sharing it via social media.

Another popular website for sharing music is Bandcamp. Unlike SoundCloud, it can also be used to sell music. You can sell individual MP3 downloads or collections of songs as albums. You decide how much money to charge, if anything at all.

If you want to be a successful musician, you'll have to attract and keep a group of fans. Fans are listeners who are as passionate about your music as you are.

Building a fan base

Sharing your music online is just the start. To move your music career on, you'll need to build up a fan base. Having fans follow your music is important for a number of reasons. Firstly, they'll spread the word about your music by telling their friends and sharing it on their social media pages. Secondly, they'll download or buy your music, and if you perform live, they'll buy tickets to see you. They might even want things like T-shirts as souvenirs of a show!

Spreading the word

Many musicians use social media to promote their music. They use websites such as Facebook and Twitter, which allow them to set up profile pages and interact with fans. Pop stars can build up a huge army of followers on Twitter. Katy Perry, for example, is followed by more than 65 million Twitter users!

STAY SAFE

You have to be at least 13 years of age to sign up to YouTube, Twitter, Facebook and many other websites. If you're younger than this, why not get your parent or guardian's permission to sign up and ask them to post updates on your behalf?

Try to create a website to promote your music. You could include the following:

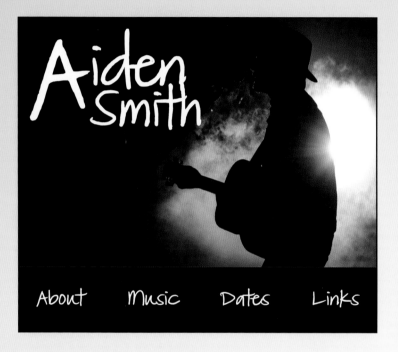

1. About: This page can explain a bit more about you, your band and your music.

2. Music: This could take visitors to songs or videos that you've uploaded to SoundCloud or YouTube.

3. Dates: This could contain details of any gigs you have coming up and how to get tickets for them.

4. Links: Include links to any social media profile pages you have created for the band, so fans can follow you.

Just the beginning!

After reading this book, you should now have a better idea of how to make, write and record your own songs. There are so many possibilities after that. For example, you can share your songs online or perform them in front of crowds. It's a lot to take in, but that's the thing about music: it's not so much a hobby as an obsession for life!

Careers in the music industry

Not everyone who makes music can become an international pop star, but that doesn't stop people from making music their life. There are plenty of other careers for musicians and music producers. For example, you could become a session musician for hire, playing guitar, piano or drums on other people's songs. Alternatively, you could work in a music studio, play your instrument in an orchestra, or compose music for film or television. If you enjoy listening to different kinds of music, you could become a reviewer and write about other people's performances for a living. Or perhaps you want to promote concerts for a job?

Even if you don't pursue a career in music, you'll still be hooked for life. Once you've got the music bug, there's no going back!

Success Story

One of today's biggest pop stars started young. Taylor Swift has been singing since she was a child. Her life changed when she started writing songs and playing the guitar at the age of twelve. She soon began performing live. By the time she was seventeen, Taylor had recorded her first hit song.

One day you could be following in the footsteps of your musical heroes, playing concerts in stadiums to thousands of your adoring fans!

Glossary

application (app) piece of computer software designed for a specific purpose, such as recording music

chord three or more musical notes, played simultaneously, which sound good together

chord sequence arrangement of chords into some kind of ear-pleasing order, which can then be performed or recorded

electronic dance music style of fast-tempo music made by computers and their software or possibly involving synthesizers and keyboards

encore additional performance at the end of a concert. When a band finishes a gig and walks offstage, if the audience shouts for more they will come out and perform an encore of songs. Encore literally means "more" in French.

fan enthusiastic supporter of something, for example of a singer, band or sports team

fan base collective term for a musician or band's fans

harmony musical notes and performances that sound good together. If two or more people are singing together perfectly in tune, or are singing notes that make up a chord, they are said to be in harmony.

instrumental anything made using instruments, or pieces of music without singing. Many classical or dance tracks, are said to be instrumental.

interface part of a computer program that allows a user to access different functions on it

jazz style of music first made popular by black American musicians in the early 20th century. Jazz music often features heavy drum rhythms and brass instruments such as trumpets, trombones and saxophones.

loop repeating sound, melody, chord, riff or drumbeat

lyrics words to a song

note single musical sound. On a piano, each of the keys plays a separate note.

pop short for "popular music". Pop music is so called because it is popular with a much larger number of people than many other styles. Pop songs are usually designed to be attractive to a wide range of listeners.

producer someone who makes music with the aid of a computer or other electronic equipment, or specializes in recording and producing other people's music

record label company that specializes in the recording, distribution, marketing and sales of recorded music

rhythm strong, repeated pattern of sound, for example a drumbeat

riff repeated pattern in music, for example a chord sequence or melody. Guitar riffs are popular in rock music.

sample portion of a sound recording, for example a set of notes, chords or a drumbeat. Producers often use samples while creating instrumental music or songs.

session musician person who is hired to play an instrument for various recording sessions or events. They are not part of a set band.

take during the recording process, a take is a single run-through of a song by a singer, musician or band. If a band completes a song in one take, that means that the recording of the performance was perfect first time.

vinyl record pressed black discs featuring music "pressed" into the surface. Before CDs and downloads, records or cassette tapes were the most popular formats for buying recorded music. Many people still listen to vinyl records.

vocal singing, speaking, rapping or other sounds made with the mouth during performing or recording music

Find out more

Books

Finding a Music Style (I'm in the Band), Adam Miller (Raintree, 2014)
Forming a Band (I'm in the Band), Richard Spilsbury (Raintree, 2014)
Performing Live (The Music Scene), Matt Anniss (Franklin Watts, 2015)
Recording and Promoting Your Music (I'm in the Band), Matt Anniss
    (Raintree, 2015)
Start a Band! (Find Your Talent), Matt Anniss (Franklin Watts, 2012)

Websites

Classics for Kids
www.classicsforkids.com
Whether or not you know much about classical music, this website is well
worth a visit. It features loads of great information and activities, including a
game where you can compose your own music.

Music Theory
www.musictheory.net
If you're interested in learning more about how to play and compose music,
this tablet-friendly site is ideal. It features interactive music lessons and
much more.

Virtual Keyboard
**www.bgfl.org/bgfl/custom/resources_ftp/client_ftp/ks2/music/
piano/strings.htm**
Play a virtual piano – both melodies and chords – by clicking on the screen.
You can change the sound, try different chords and even play along to
different drumbeats!

World Music Composer
www.nms.ac.uk/explore/play/world-music-composer
Learn about different instruments and musical styles from around the world,
then try to make your own music with them.

Further research

Whatever aspect of music making, recording or performance you're most interested in, you'll be able to find useful information online. There are some great links to websites aimed at giving advice to young musicians. You can also find loads of free music lessons and tips, in the form of videos on sites like YouTube.

If you're interested in playing music with others, there may be school bands and orchestras that you can join. If you want to take it a little more seriously, there could well be bands and orchestras that represent your town, city or region. You normally have to try out for these to show them that you can play your chosen instrument to a good standard. If you're more interested in doing things yourself, you could start your own band at school. If you need bandmates, put up a poster on the school noticeboard, asking would-be musicians to get in touch.

Many recording studios and local music charities offer children and young people free courses in music production and recording. These will give you an introduction to the recording process, and help you learn the basics of using Digital Audio Workstation (DAW) software. Recording studios sometimes offer free time for up-and-coming bands to record, too. Visit your local music shop to find out more.

If you enjoy comparing and contrasting music more than playing it, try starting your own blog. You could review songs from new bands, recommend music that your friends don't yet know about, or post links to great music videos you've found online. If you're under 13, you may need to get a parent or guardian to post for you.

Index